3

Lehrwerk für den Englischunterricht ab Klasse 3

Activity Book 3 Förderheft

Erarbeitet von
Jasmin Brune
Daniela Elsner
Stefanie Gleixner-Weyrauch
Simone Gutwerk
Martina Koch
Marion Lugauer
Sabine Schwarz

Auf der Grundlage der Ausgabe von
Martina Bredenbröcker, Jasmin Brune, Daniela Elsner,
Barbara Gleich, Stefanie Gleixner-Weyrauch, Simone Gutwerk,
Marion Lugauer, Sabine Schwarz, Anke Spangenberg

Unter Beratung von Jane Brockmann-Fairchild

Portfolio: Nina Thelen

Illustriert von
Barbara Jung, Wilfried Poll,
Gisela Vogel, Thilo Pustlauk, Anja Boretzki

Inhalt

What's your name?

1  **Read and write.**

Hello, my name is Sally. What's your name?

My name is
_____.

2 **Draw a picture of yourself or stick in a photo.**

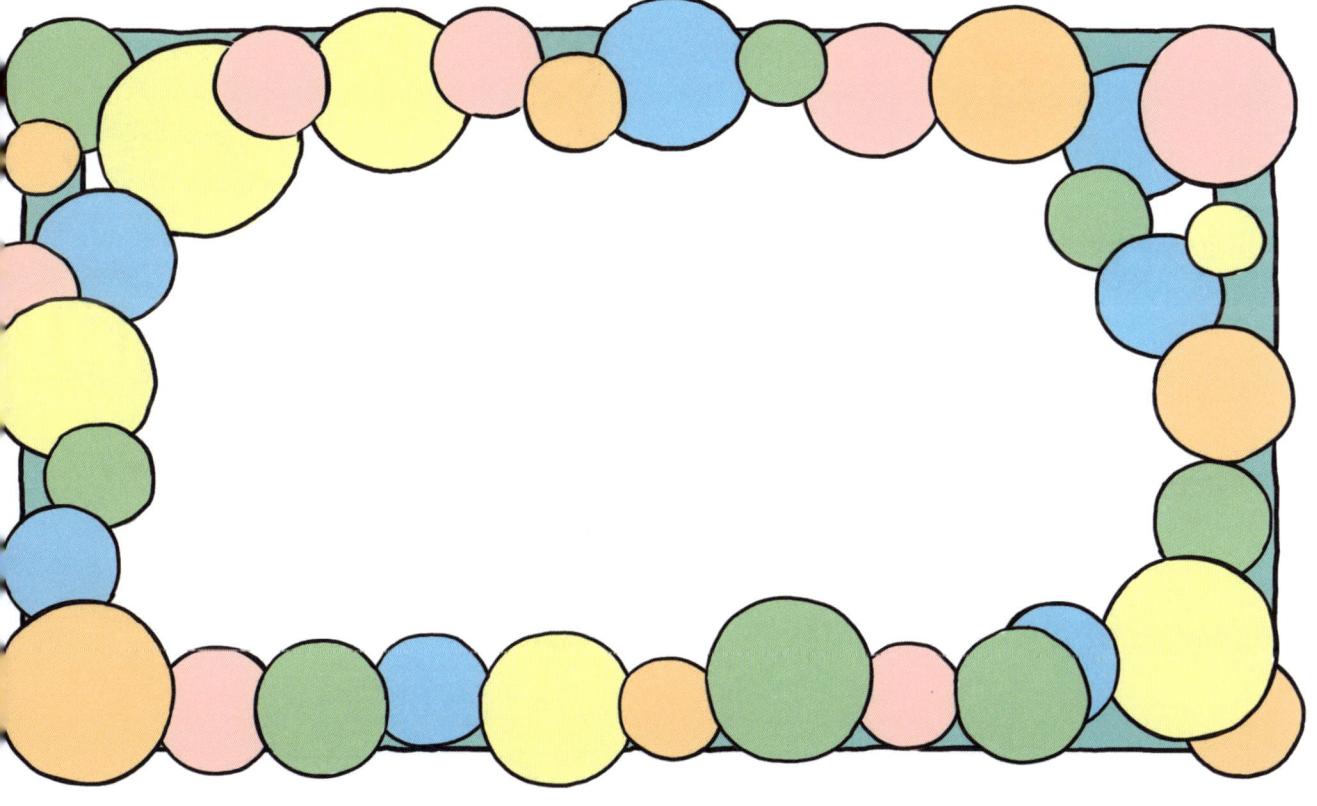

3 **Ask your partner:** What's your name?

Hello

Who is it?

1 🔘 **Listen.**

2 ✏️ **Draw lines and write.**

Hi, I'm Susan.

I like **tennis**.

Hello, my name is Tim.

I like **computer games**.

Hi, my name is Phil.

I like **basketball**.

Good morning, I'm Eric.

I like my **skateboard**.

Hello, I'm Emily.

I like **singing**.

Hi, my name is Liz.

I like **inline skating**.

Hello, I'm Sally and I ♥ lollipops.

💬 **And you? What do you like?**

3 ✏️ **Fill in your portfolio.**

What colour is it?

1  **Colour and write.**

g r e e n   o r a n g e   p i n k

g r e y   p u r p l e   b r o w n

What colour am I?

2  **Listen to the song and colour. Write the text.**

◯ + ◯ , ◯ + ◯ , ◯ + ◯ . (2 x)

Red and yellow, blue and green, blue and green.

And ◯ + ◯ + ◯ + ◯ .

And brown and black and white and grey.

◯ + ◯ , ◯ + ◯ , ◯ + ◯ .

R_____ and y_____ , b_____ and g_____ , b_____ and g_____ .

Ten kangaroos

1 🖊 **Draw lines.**

2 💿🖍 **Listen and colour.**

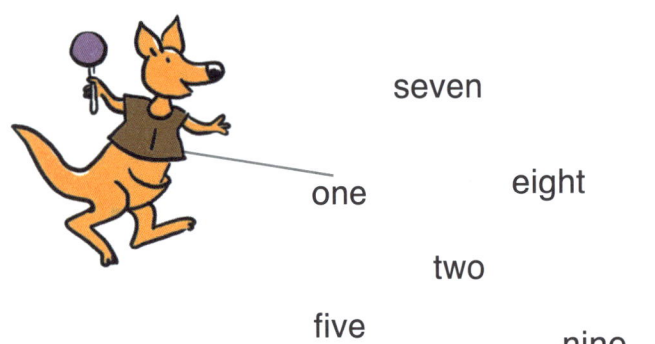

seven

one

two

five

ten

eight

three

six

nine

four

What's your telephone number?

My telephone number is

_____

_____.

3 💿🖊 **Listen and write.**

Emily

| | 9 | 8 | |

Tim and Susan

Phil

4 🦘 **Make a telephone list. Ask your friends.**

⭐ **Do you know other important telephone numbers?**

5 🖊 **Fill in your portfolio.**

police …
school …
Dad's mobile …
Mum's mobile …

School things

1 🖉 **Number and write.**

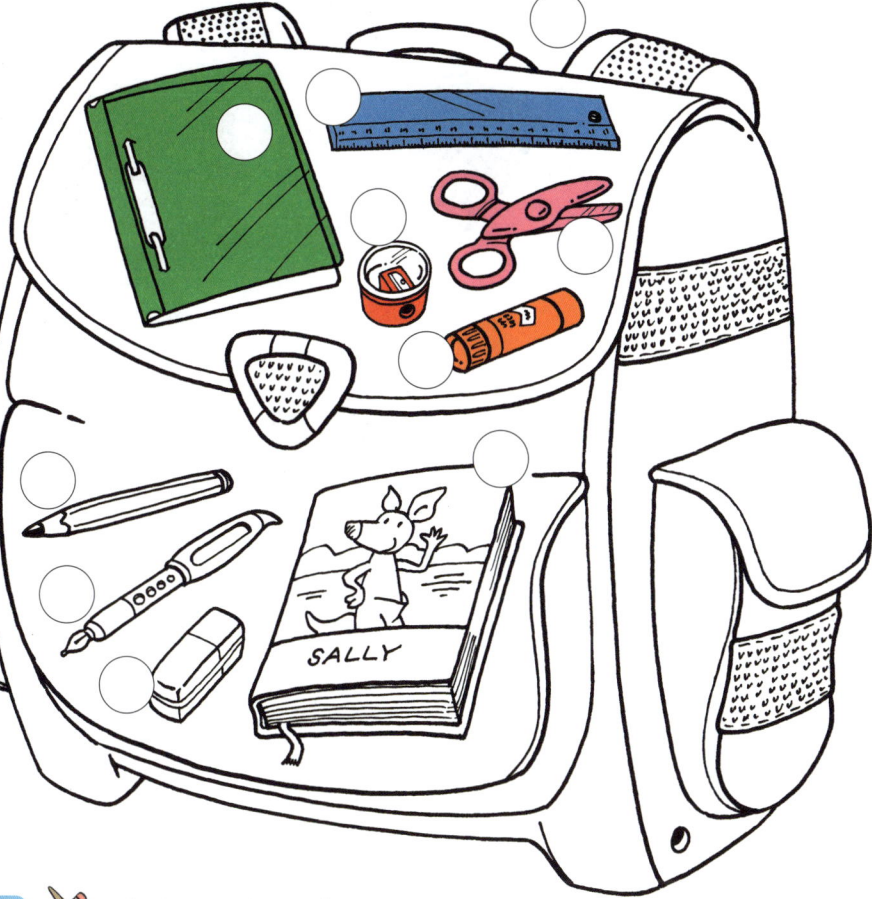

1 ruler

2 folder

3 glue stick

4 scissors

5 pencil sharpener

6 **rubber**

7 **pencil**

8 **pen**

9 **book**

10 **schoolbag**

2 🖌 **Colour the pictures.**

3 👥 **Tell your partner:** My ruler is blue.

4 🖉 **Do the crossword.**

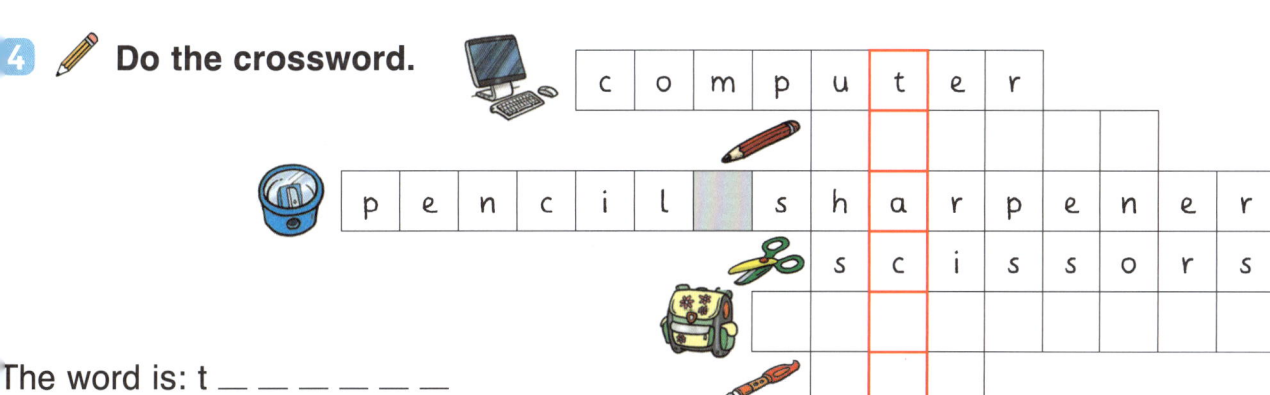

| c | o | m | p | u | t | e | r | | |

| p | e | n | c | i | l | | s | h | a | r | p | e | n | e | r |

s | c | i | s | s | o | r | s

The word is: t _ _ _ _ _ _

5 👥 **Talk to your partner about your own school things:**
I've got a green pen. And you?

Where are the school things?

1  **Draw lines.**

The pencil case is **under** the schoolbag.

The rubber is **in** the pencil case.

The glue stick is **on** the book.

in

on

under

2  **Read and draw.**

The pencil is on the book.

The ruler is under the folder.

3  **Look at the pictures and write.**

The book is _____ the schoolbag.

The book is _____ the schoolbag.

4  **Write and colour.**

The book is _____

the _____ .

5  **Fill in your portfolio.**

The body

1 ✏️ **Number and write.**

◯ knees ◯ eyes

◯ toes ① ears

◯ shoulders ◯ head

◯ mouth ◯ nose

Ouch!

2 **Write your own comic. Act it out.**

Good morning, Sally. Here is your tea.

I can't go to school.

Ouch! My
_____.

Let me see.

Ouch! My
_____.

Let me see.

Go to school.

Get up, Susan!

1 💿 Listen.

2 ✏️ Write the words.

3 ✂️ 🖇️ Cut out the pictures (page 47), match and stick in.

Stretch your arms.

Stretch your legs.

Shake your hands.

Shake your fingers.

Shake your feet.

Go into the bathroom.

Wash your face.

Brush your hair.

Brush your teeth.

Open your mouth.

Say: Good morning!

1 arm – 2 arms
1 leg – 2 legs

1 foot – 2 feet
1 tooth – 2 teeth

Monster, monster, how do you feel?

1 🖊 **Look and write.**

The monster is _____.

The monster is tired .

The monster is scared .

The monster is _____.

_____
_____

sad   angry   s̶c̶a̶r̶e̶d̶
fine   happy   t̶i̶r̶e̶d̶   okay

And I feel
fine!

2 🖊 **How do you feel? Write.**

I'm _____.

If you're happy

1. If you're hap-py and you know it, clap your hands.
   If you're hap-py and you know it, clap your hands.
   If you're hap-py and you know it and you real-ly want to show it,
   if you're hap-py and you know it, clap your hands.

1  **Listen and write.**

2 ✏️ **Draw lines.**

If you're happy and you know it,

       clap your hands ...

       stamp your feet ...

       snap your fingers ...

       say: we are ...

       do it all ...

3 ✏️ **Now it's your turn. Write.**

If you're _____ and you know it,

_____

_____

angry   scared

4 ✏️ **Fill in your portfolio.**

sad   tired

The fish who could wish

1 **Listen and tick ✔. Write the words.**

 ✔

castle

car

doll

helicopter

horse

computer game

guitar

teddy bear

2  **Now it's your turn. What do you wish for? Write or draw.**

bike   skateboard   computer
football   book …

 **Toys**

What can the children buy?

£20 helicopter

spaceship

£17

helmet £30

£90 bike

helmet

£40

£100 bike
£200

castle £80 £10 doll

£18 football

£8

racing car book

£1 rubber £5

£2 £3

ruler pencils

£10
+£5
+£2
+£2
+£1
=£20

£10
+£2
=£12

£10
+£5
+£1
+£1
+ 50 p
+ 20 p
+ 10 p
+ 10 p
+ 10 p
= £18

1 ✏ **Write.**

	wish	How much is it?	money 🐷	yes	no
Tim	racing car	£ 18	£ 20	✔	
Emily	c _ _ _ _ _	£	£		
Susan	d _ _ _	£	£		

2 💬 **Say:** Tim wants the racing car. It's 18 pounds. He has got 20 pounds.

Emily wants … It's … She has got …

3 ✏ **What do you want? Write.**

I want _____

_____

_____

4 ✏ **Fill in your portfolio.**

Sally in the snow

1 🖉 **Read, write and number.**

⑥ Sally puts on her **scarf**.

⑧ Sally puts on her **gloves**.

② Sally puts on her **trousers**.

◯ Sally puts on her **woolly hat**.

◯ Sally puts on her **boots**.

◯ Sally puts on her T-shirt

and her socks.

◯ Sally puts on her pullover.

◯ Sally puts on her jacket.

2 🖉 **What is Sally wearing? Write.**

Sally is wearing her scarf, her woolly hat,

her gloves, her _____

_____

_____

 **Clothes**

My clothes

1 🖊 **Match the pictures and the words. Write.**

a pair of trousers   T-shirt   jacket   pullover

a pair of jeans

coat

shirt

shoes

dress

a pair of shorts

cap

skirt

gloves   socks   scarf   woolly hat   boots

2 🖊 **Winter or summer holidays? Pack your suitcase and write.**

For my summer holidays, I pack
a T-shirt, a pair of shorts,
a pair of jeans, a cap, shoes,
socks.
Girls: a skirt, a dress

For my winter holidays, I pack
_____
_____
_____
_____
_____

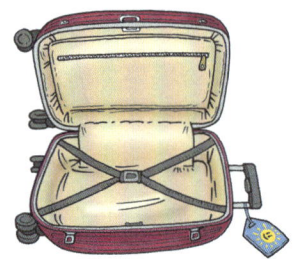 

3 🖊 **Fill in your portfolio.**

When can we meet?

1 💿 ✏️ **When can the children meet? Listen and draw lines.**

Hi. Let's meet on _____.
Susan

Monday   Friday   Saturday
Wednesday   Tuesday
Thursday   Sunday

2 ✏️ **Write the days in the correct order.**

1 _____   2 Tuesday   3 _____

4 Thursday   5 _____   6 Saturday

7 _____

3 👥 **Work in groups. Find out when you can meet.**

name	Mon	Tue	Wed	Thu	Fri	Sat	Sun

 Can we meet on Monday/...?   Yes, we can. ✔

○ We can meet on _____.

No, we can't. —

○ We can't meet.

The wind and the sun

1 💿 **Listen.**

2 ✂️ 🖊️ **Cut out the speech bubbles (page 47), match and stick in.**

I'm stronger than you.

I can make the man take off his coat. I'm the strongest.

3 👦👧 **Read the speech bubbles with your partner.**

4 ✏️ **Write.**

strong

stronger

strongest

strong
stronger
strongest

What's the weather like?

1  **Listen and write the weather words.**

Hi there. This is **Tim** from London with the weather forecast. It's another foggy and _____ day. So stay at home.

Good morning from Rome. This is **Emily** with the weather forecast. It's _____ and sunny . Don't forget your suncream.

Hi, this is **Susan** with the weather forecast from Istanbul. Today it's _____ and very windy . Hold on to your hats.

Good morning, this is **Eric** from Berlin. Here's the weather forecast. It's cloudy and snowy . Put on your boots.

cloudy   cold   foggy   hot   rainy   snowy   sunny   windy

2 **Make your own weather forecast. Write and draw.**

Hello. This is ═══════════════════════

from ═══════════════════════════════

Today it's ═══════════════ and ═══════════════ .

3 **Fill in your portfolio.**

Happy birthday

1 🖊 **Read and write.**

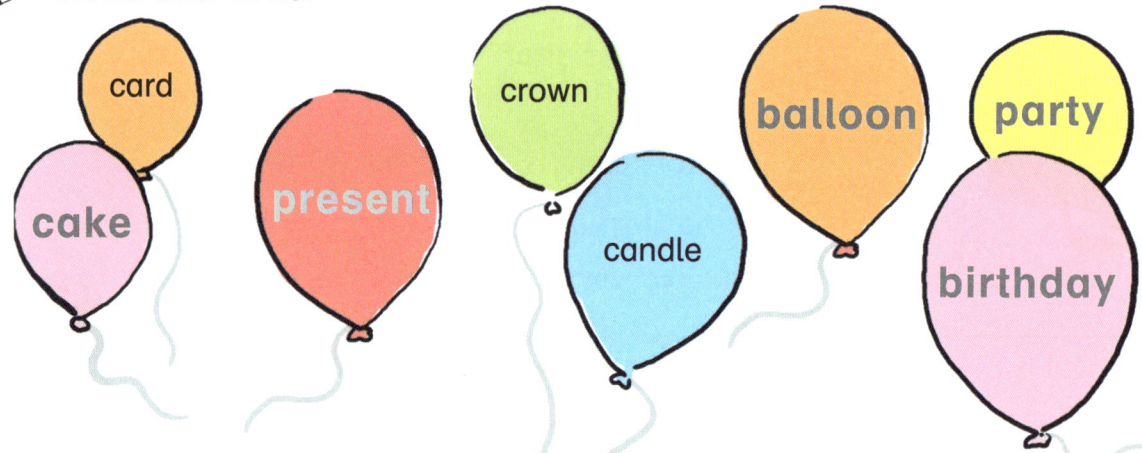

card

cake

present

crown

candle

balloon

party

birthday

2 🖊 **Spot the 8 differences.**

3 🖊 **How old are you?** I'm _____ .

When's your birthday? My birthday is in _____ .

Seasons and months

1 🖊 **Read and write.**

2 🖊 **Write the correct months under each picture.**

In winter

I like the ❄ snow and ice

and Christmas Day. All this is nice.

December, January,

February

In _____ I like the flowers,

🥚🥚 Easter eggs

and April showers.

March, April, May

In _____ I like Halloween,

the 👻 ghosts

and witches I have seen.

September, October,

November

In _____

I like the ☀ sun,

the holidays and lots of fun!

June, July, August

summer   spring   winter   autumn

3 🖊 **Fill in your portfolio.**

Best friends

1 💿 ✏️ **Listen and draw lines.**

Susan

Tim

Emily

Phil

Eric

Liz

2 ✏️ **Look and write.**

Susan's best friend is _____ .

Tim's best friend is _____ .

Emily's _____ .

And who is your best friend? My _____ .

> Who is it?

> He has got short brown hair.
> He is wearing a grey cap.

> She has got long blond hair.
> She is wearing a green pullover.

3 🧒👩 **Describe your friend. Write. Talk to your partner.**

He/She is a _____ . He/She is _____ years old.

He/She has got _____ hair and _____ eyes.

He/She is wearing a _____

_____
_____ .

⭐ **Can you describe other people?**

| girl boy blond black red brown |
| blue pink purple white green |
| yellow grey pullover shirt T-shirt |

he   she

My family

1 🖊 **Find the words.**

mothermumgrandfatherbrotherauntsisterfatherunclegrandmagrandpa

2 🖊 **Do the crossword.**

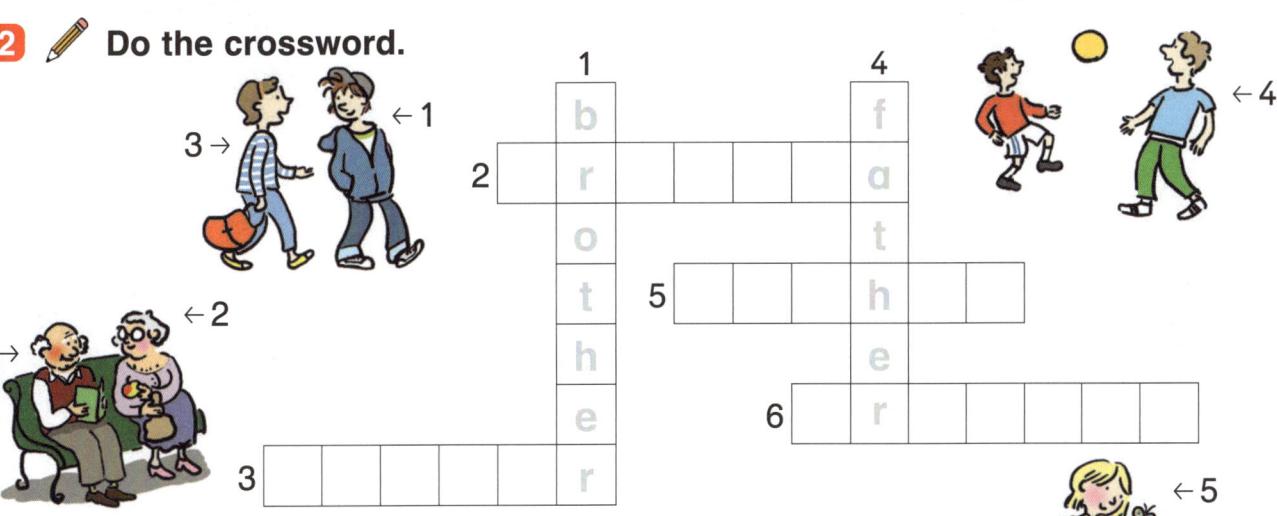

```
        1           4
        b           f
    2   r           a
        o           t
        t       5   h
        h           e
        e       6   r
3       r
```

3 💿 🖊 **Listen and point. Fill in the missing words.**

I've got a mother,

a father and a brother.

I've got a _____ and two brothers .

I haven't got a father or a sister .

I've got a mother and a _____

and a sister .

I've got a mother and a father

and a _____ and a _____ .

💬 **And you? Have you got brothers or sisters?**

It's magic

1  **Who says the magic spells? Listen and draw lines.**

> Abracadabra, one and two,
> there's a goldfish in the shoe.

> Abracadabra, one and two,
> there's a cat in the shoe.

> Bubble, bubble, trick and track,
> sister Marnie is right back.

2 **Write your own magic family spell.**

Abracadabra, one and two,
there's my _____ in the shoe.

Bubble, bubble, trick and track,
please, give me my _____ back

Abracadabra, one, two, three,
_____ come to me.

Bubble, bubble, nine and ten,
_____ is back here again.

| mother | father | sister | brother | grandma | grandpa |

_____

_____

_____

_____

3 **Fill in your portfolio.**

My favourite drink

1 ✏️ **What can you see in the mirror? Write.**

coffee

orange juice   milk

lemonade   [ ]   [ ]   [ ]

water   tea   ~~milk~~   coke   hot chocolate   ~~coffee~~   ~~orange juice~~   ~~lemonade~~

2 ✏️ **Hot drink or cold drink? Make a list.**

hot	cold
coffee, _____	coke, _____
_____	_____
_____	_____
_____	_____

3 ✏️ **Read and answer.**

What drinks do you like?   🙂   I like _____

_____.

What drink do you like best?   🙂🙂   I like _____ best.

What drinks don't you like?   🙁   I don't like _____

_____.

4 ✏️ **Fill in your portfolio.**

Food and drinks for breakfast

1 🖊 **Draw lines.**

ham   cheese   tea   honey   coffee

milk   toast   jam   bread   orange juice

butter   water   roll   egg   cornflakes

2 🖊 **Find the words.**

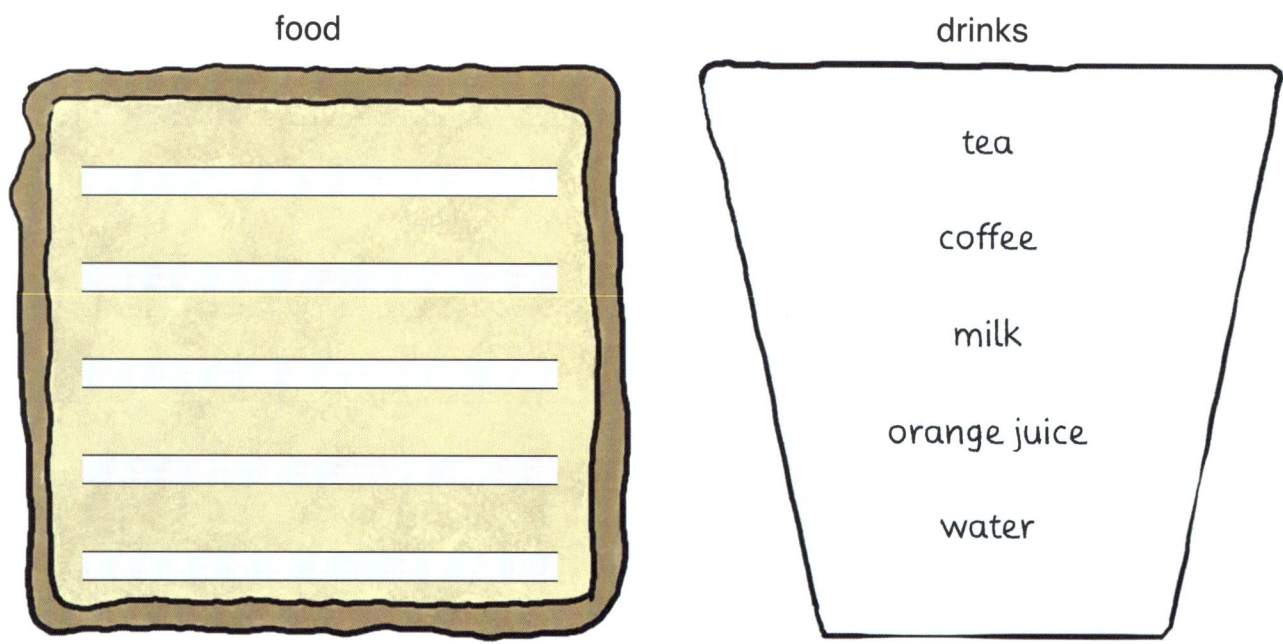

honeyrolljam
coffeeteacheese
buttermilkeggwater
breadtoastrollham
cornflakeseggbreadtea

3 🖊 **Food or drink? Fill in.**

food

drinks

tea

coffee

milk

orange juice

water

⭐ **Do you know more food or drink words? Tell your partner.**

What do you have for breakfast?

1 ✏️ **Look at the children. What do they have for breakfast?**

Eric has cornflakes and _____ .

Emily has hot chocolate and _____

and _____ .

and _____ .

Liz has a roll , _____ and _____ .

2 ✂️✏️ **Fill your plate, your glass and your cup.**

For breakfast, I have

_____ and

_____ and

_____ .

3 ✏️ **What do the children say?**

I have   Can   the   🍼   please?

Can   I have   the milk ,   please?

the   🥣   I have   Can   please?

Can I have _____

please?   the   🧈   I have   Can

_____

Can   please?   the   🍯   I have

_____

4 ✏️ **Fill in your portfolio.**

Fruit mix

1 ✎ 🖊 **Write and colour.**

a | p | i | n | e | a | p | p | l | e

a | c | h | e | r | r | y

an | | | | |

| | | | | | |

What's missing?
Draw the fruit and write.

It's a _____ .

a cherry – **a b**anana
an apple – **an o**range

2 💿 **Listen and number.**

3 💿 🖊 **Listen and tick ✔: yes or no?**

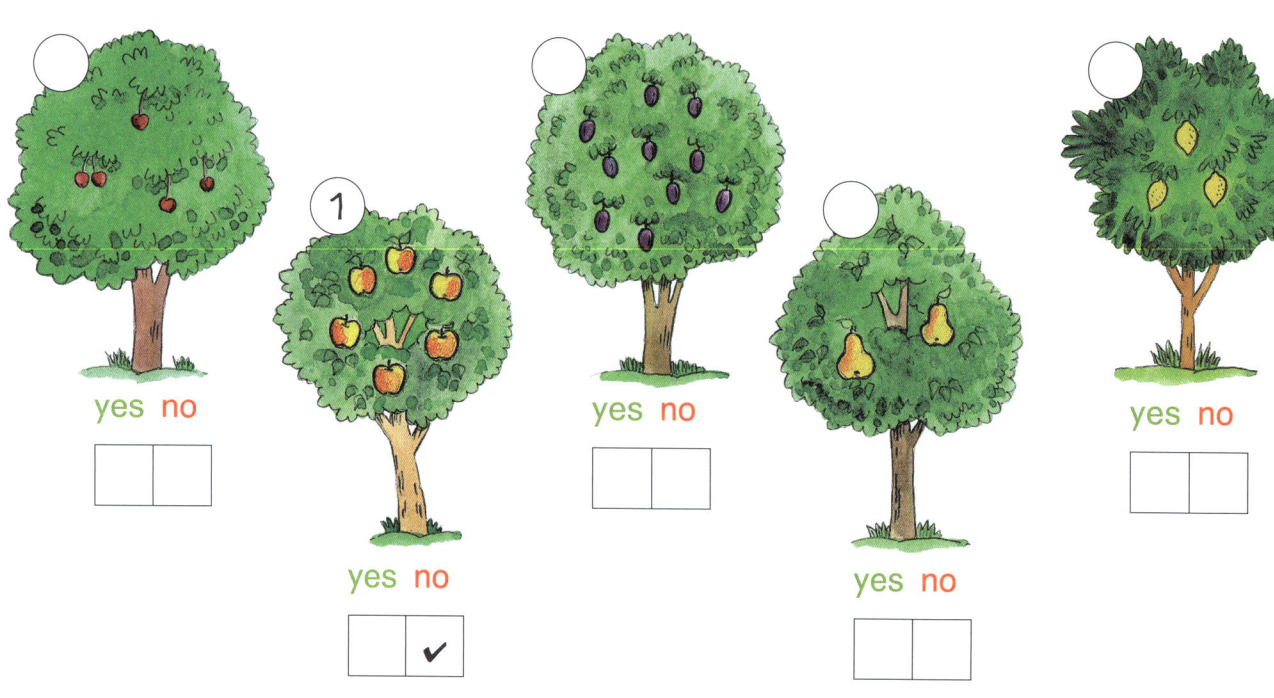

yes no

1 yes no ✔

yes no

yes no

yes no

At the ice cream stand

1  **What does Emily buy? Listen and tick ✔.**
What does Phil buy? Listen and tick ✔.

pear ☐ banana lemon ☐ strawberry ☐ cherry ☐

Pineapple orange ☐ vanilla chocolate

2 🖉 **Fill in the speech bubbles. Act out the dialogue.**

Hello.

_____ .
Can I help you?

Yes. I'd like
two scoops, please,
_____
and _____ .

Here you are. That's
£ _____ , please.

Here you are.

Thank you. Goodbye.

_____ .

3 ✂️🖉 **What would you like? Write and colour.**

I'd like _____ .

Ice cream rock

1 💿 ✏️ **Listen to the song. Look and write.**

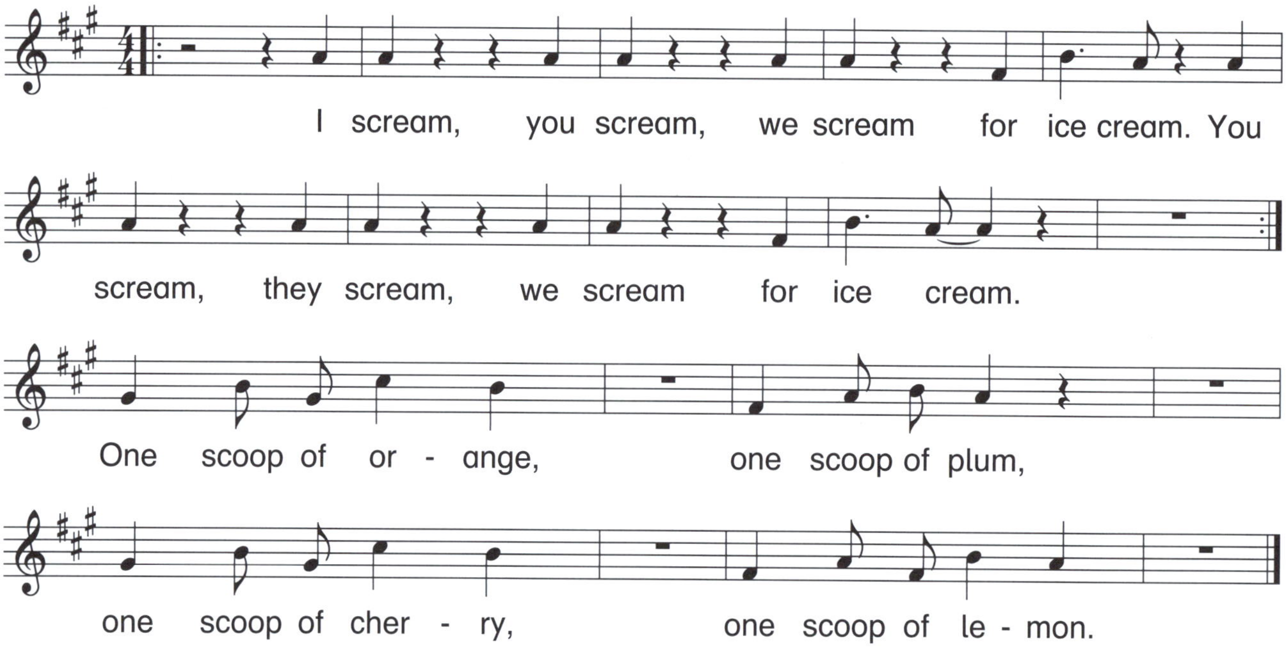

I scream, you scream, we scream for ice cream. You

scream, they scream, we scream for ice cream.

One scoop of or - ange, one scoop of plum,

one scoop of cher - ry, one scoop of le - mon.

One scoop of  _____, one scoop of _____,

one scoop of  cherry , one scoop of  lemon .

One scoop of _____, one scoop of  pear ,

one scoop of _____, one scoop of  melon .

apple   orange   melon   pear   plum   cherry   chocolate
lemon   banana   pineapple   strawberry   vanilla

2 ✏️ **Now it's your turn. Write.**

One scoop of _____, one scoop of _____

_____ .

3 ✏️ **Fill in your portfolio.**

Our pets

1 ✏️ **Do the crossword.**

		g				
m	o	u				
		i				
		n		c		
		e				r
		a				
		p				
f	i	g			b	u	d	g	i	e
		g				

budgie cat dog
fish ~~guinea pig~~
hamster mouse
rabbit

2 ✏️ **What's your favourite pet?**

My favourite pet is a

_____ .

Its name is

_____ .

It is _____ .

It is _____ .

black brown grey
white big small …

3 ✏️ **Draw your favourite pet.**

⭐ **Find more pets in your dictionary.**
Describe them to your partner.

Little dog lost

1

2

I've got an idea.

I've found a little dog.

3

Animal Centre

4

Let's go to the animal centre.

5

6

1 Listen.

2 ✂️ Cut out the speech bubbles (page 49), match and stick in.

Lost pets

1 🖊 **Read and number.**

cat grey and white green eyes `1`	`7`

rabbit white, red eyes We miss Roger very much! `2`	 

tortoise green and brown small head `3`

two guinea pigs brown and white `4`

hamster brown and yellow `5`

 `7`

budgie blue with a yellow head `6`

three mice small grey, white and black `7`

1 dog – 2 dogs
1 cat – 2 cats

1 mouse – 2 mice
1 fish – 2 fish

2 ✂ **What's missing? Draw the pets.**

3 ✂ **Read and colour.**

4 🖊 **Fill in your portfolio.**

thirty-three **33**

At Madame Tussaud's

1 🔘 ✏️ **Listen and number.**

2 ✏️ **Tick ✔ the correct answer.**

The tickets are   £60. ✔

      £18. ☐

      £20. ☐

Tim wants to see   Schwarzenegger. ☐

         Mozart. ☐

         Johnny Depp. ☐

Susan loves   Prince William. ☐

     Kate's dress. ☐

     Prince Harry. ☐

I want to see Big Ben.

3 ✏️ **What do you want to see in London? Look in a book or on the Internet.**

I want to see _____ .

On the farm

1 🖉 **Look and write.**

goose

pig

sheep

cow

hen

horse

duck

duck ~~hen~~ ~~goose~~ ~~pig~~ cow sheep horse

in   on   under   in front of   next to   behind

2 🖉 **Where are the animals? Write.**

The goose is on the 🔺 .

The pig is _____ the 🏠 .

The hen is _____ the 🪑 .

The _____ is next to the 🪑 .

The _____ is behind the 🌳 .

The _____ is in the 🌊 .

The _____ is in front of the 🏡 .

I know an old lady ...

1 ✂️ 🖊️ **Make your own story. Cut out the animals (page 49) and stick in.**

2 🖊️ **Write your story.**

I know an old lady who swallowed a _____

and a _____ and a _____.

And then? She sneezed – of course.

dog hen mouse fly pig cat
cow sheep fish duck goose

3 **Read your story.**

4 🖊️ **Fill in your portfolio.**

Robin Hood's clever trick

1 🔴 ✏️ **Listen and read the speech bubbles. Draw lines.**

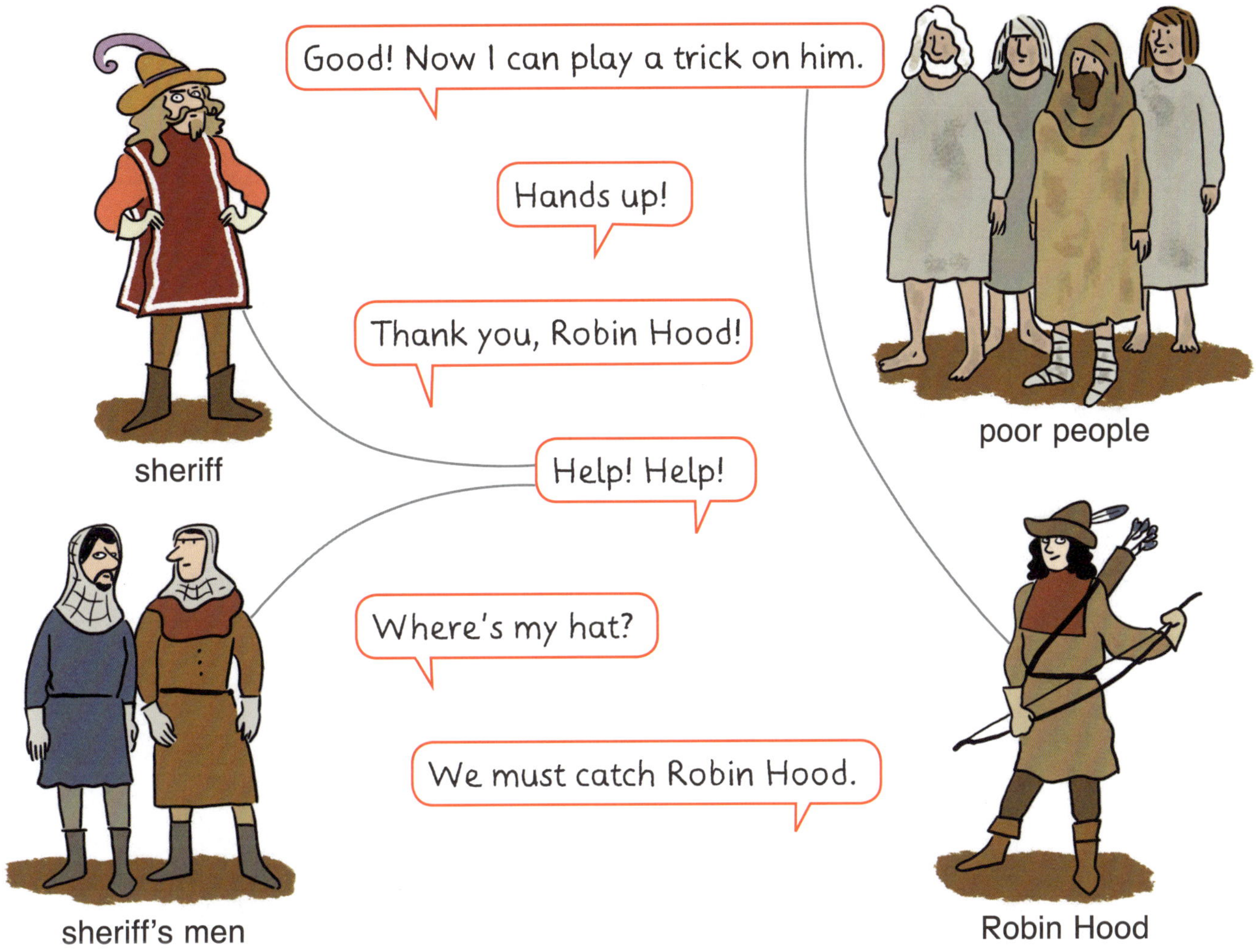

Good! Now I can play a trick on him.

Hands up!

Thank you, Robin Hood!

sheriff

poor people

Help! Help!

Where's my hat?

We must catch Robin Hood.

sheriff's men

Robin Hood

2 ✏️ **True or false? Read and tick ✔.**

	true	false
Robin Hood lives in a castle.		✔
The sheriff is a good man.		
The sheriff wants to catch Robin Hood.		
Robin Hood plays a trick on the sheriff.		
Robin Hood shoots with his bow and arm.		✔
The sheriff is wearing a woolly hat.		
The sheriff is riding a cow.		
Robin Hood gives clothes to the poor.	✔	

Let's talk

1 ✂️ 🖍️ Cut out the speech bubbles 💬 (page 49). Match and stick in.

2 ✏️ Write more dialogues.

3 👦👧 Act out the dialogues with a partner.

> What's your name?

> My telephone numb[er]
> is 638215.

> How are you?
>
> I'm fine, thanks.

> How much
> is the ruler?
>
> It's £ 2.

> My birthday is in May.

Birthdays in our class

January	February	March
April	May	June
July	August	September
November		

> How old are you?

Have you got brothers or sisters?

What drinks do you like?

Do you like butter on your bread?

Can I help you?

Yes, I'd like 2 apples, please.

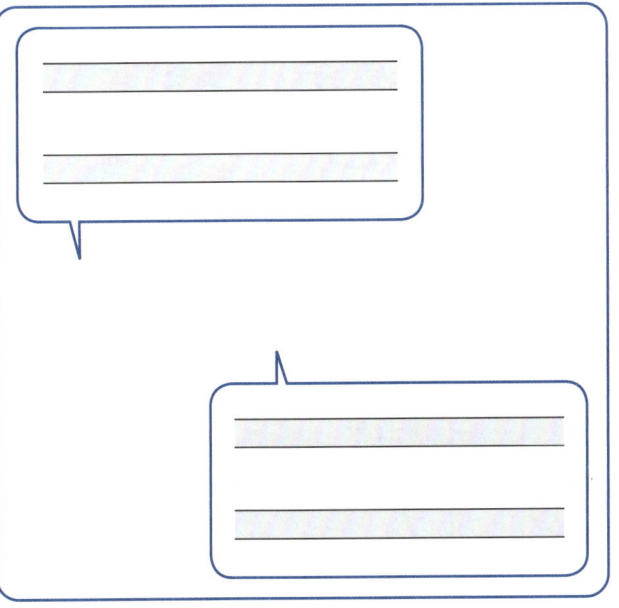

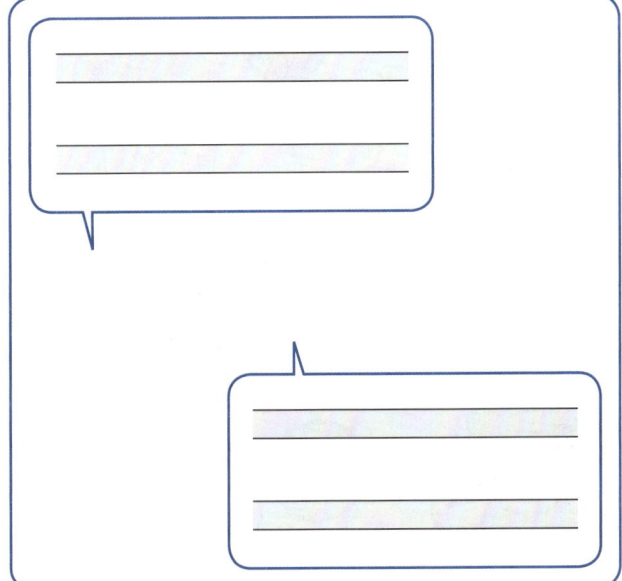

Board game

1. ✏ Fill in the speech bubbles.

2. Play the game with your friends.

🎲 Roll the dice. Take turns.

🗨 If you land on a speech bubble, answer the question.

Move one field forward.

Move one field backward.

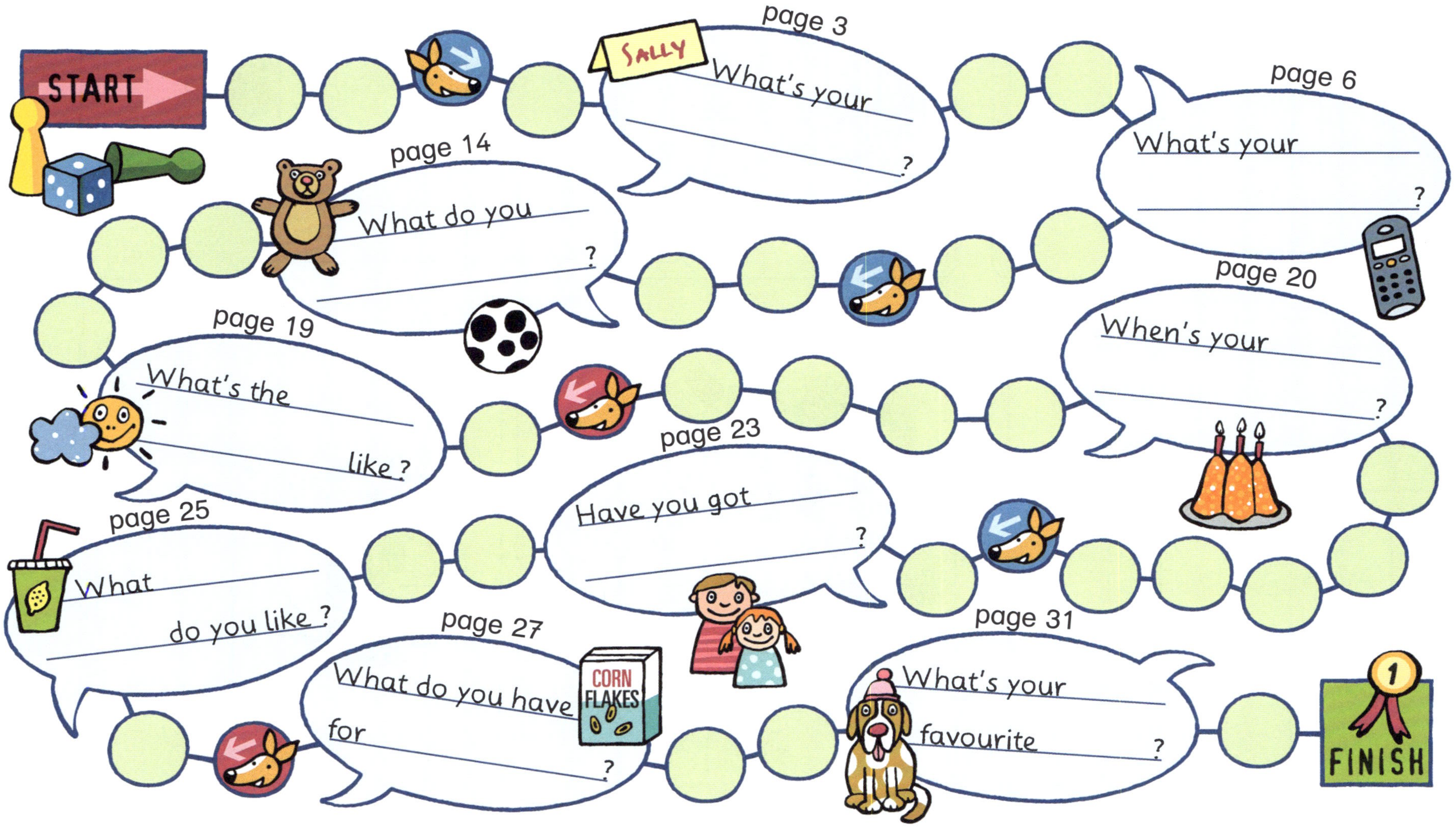

START

page 14

What do you _____ ?

page 19

What's the _____ like ?

page 25

What do you like _____ ?

page 27

What do you have _____ for _____ ?

page 23

Have you got _____ ?

page 3

What's your _____ ? — Sally

page 31

What's your favourite _____ ?

page 20

When's your _____ ?

page 6

What's your _____ ?

FINISH

It's Halloween

1  **Listen and match.**

2 💿 ✏️ **Listen and circle** ◯ **the parts of the body.**

3 💿 ✏️ **Find Emily's costume. Listen and tick ✔.**

☐

☐

4 ✏️ 👦👧 **Draw your own Halloween costume and tell your partner.**

Trick or treat,
trick or treat.

On Halloween,
I'm a _____.

A chubby little snowman

A chubby little
has a carrot
along jumps
and what do you suppose?

That hungry little kangaroo,
looking for her lunch,
eats the snowman's nose,
nibble, nibble, CRUNCH!

1 💿 **Listen.**

2 ✂️ **Cut out the rhyme (page 51), find the correct order and stick in.**

3 ✏️ **Draw pictures.**

4 💬 **Learn the rhyme.**

Christmas Eve

1 🔘 ✏️ **Listen and number.**

( ) stocking   (3) presents   (5) Christmas cards

(1) bed   ( ) reindeer   ( ) Father Christmas

2 ✏️ **Draw lines.**

Christmas tree   chimney   sleigh   present

reindeer   Father Christmas   stocking

Hurry, Santa!

3 🔘 ✏️ **Listen, read and correct the sentences.**

It is ~~Halloween~~.

It is Christmas Eve.

~~Grandpa~~ puts on his clothes.

Santa _____

Go, ~~kangaroo,~~ go!

_____

That ~~schoolbag~~ is for you.

_____

stocking   mistletoe   present   ~~Santa~~   sleigh   reindeer   ~~Christmas Eve~~

Edgar's Easter eggs

1  Listen and number.

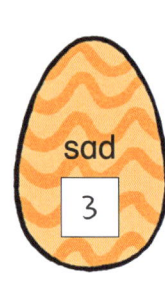 happy [ ]

 sad [3]

Easter eggs [1]

basket [ ]

colour [2]

share [ ]

2 Cut out the speech bubbles (page 51), match and stick in.

Let's hide the eggs.

But sharing is fun.

Where are the Easter eggs?

1 ✏️ **Hide your eggs. Fill in the words.**

The blue egg is in front of the bush.

The red egg is behind the fence.

The brown egg is next to the flower.

The yellow egg is _____ the tree.

The pink egg is _____ the basket.

The purple egg is _____ Edgar.

The green egg is _____ Edgar's mother.

in

on

under

next to

in front of

behind

2 ✏️ **Draw and colour the Easter eggs.**

3 👦👩 **Find your partner's Easter eggs.**

Is the blue egg under the bush?

Yes, it is.

No, it isn't.

Get up, Susan! (page 10)

 ## The wind and the sun (page 18)

No, I'm stronger than you.	
See, I'm stronger than you. I'm the strongest!	You can never do this. I can make the man take off his coat. I'm the strongest.

Little dog lost (page 32)

Thank you very much.	Mummy, where is Bobby?
Hello. Can I help you?	

I know an old lady … (page 36)

 fly	 cow	 mouse	 pig	 fish	
duck	 dog	 cat	 goose	 sheep	hen

Let's talk (page 38, 39)

My name is Jenny.	What's your telephone number?
I'm 9 years old.	When is your birthday?

No, thank you.
I like water and tea.
Yes, I've got a sister and a brother.

A chubby little snowman (page 42)

The snowman turns

from  to and Sally knows that this is bad.

Off she jumps

and hop, hop, hop,

she goes to get a  .

 ## Edgar's Easter eggs (page 44)

Beautiful eggs!

Thank you, Edgar.
You're my best friend.

Let's colour Easter eggs.

No!

Sally

Mein Sprachenportfolio
Klasse 3

My name is _____.

**So habe ich
im Englischunterricht gearbeitet:**

	1. Halbjahr	2. Halbjahr
Ich habe aufmerksam zugehört.	⬤⬤⬤	⬤⬤⬤
Ich habe mich regelmäßig gemeldet.	⬤⬤⬤	⬤⬤⬤
Ich habe versucht, neue Wörter genau nachzusprechen.	⬤⬤⬤	⬤⬤⬤
Ich habe versucht, in Gesprächen möglichst viel auf Englisch zu sagen.	⬤⬤⬤	⬤⬤⬤
Ich habe die Lieder mitgesungen.	⬤⬤⬤	⬤⬤⬤
Ich habe mindestens einen Reim gründlich geübt und aufgesagt.	⬤⬤⬤	⬤⬤⬤
Ich habe bei den Hörübungen genau zugehört.	⬤⬤⬤	⬤⬤⬤
Ich konnte verstehen, was meine Lehrerin / mein Lehrer auf Englisch sagt.	⬤⬤⬤	⬤⬤⬤
Ich habe Wörter richtig abgeschrieben.	⬤⬤⬤	⬤⬤⬤
Ich konnte schon kleine Texte schreiben.	⬤⬤⬤	⬤⬤⬤

Name: _____

Geburtstag: _____

Geburtsort: _____

Geburtsland: _____

_____

Diese Sprachen kann ich sprechen:

_____

Diese Sprachen kann ich verstehen:

_____

Diese Sprachen lerne ich in der Schule:

_____

_____

Diese Sprachen möchte ich gerne noch lernen:

_____

In diesen Ländern, in denen andere Sprachen gesprochen werden,
war ich schon einmal:

_____

_____

So habe ich mich dort verständigt:

_____

_____

1 ✏️ **Diese Wörter kenne ich schon auf Englisch:**

2 ✏️ **Ich kenne auch Wörter aus anderen Sprachen:**

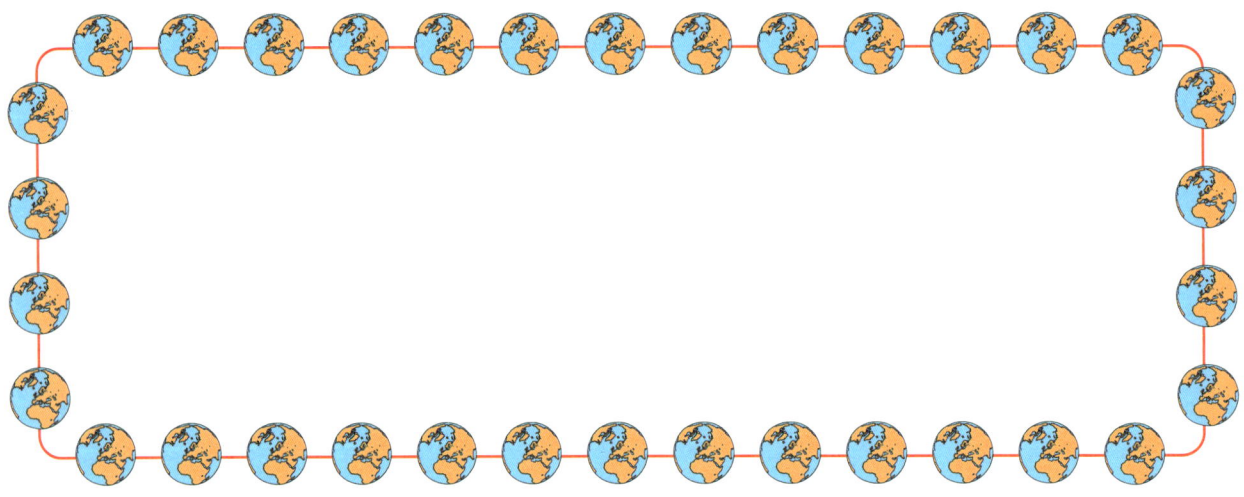

3 **Ich kann mich vorstellen und sagen, was ich mag:**

Hello, my name is _____ .

I like _____ .

4 **Das kann ich auch schon auf Englisch:**

Ich kann sagen, wie es mir geht.

Ich kann andere fragen, wie es ihnen geht.

1 ✖ ✏️ **Diese Farben kann ich benennen und aufschreiben:**

Male die Kleckse in verschiedenen Farben aus.

Hilfe findest du im Activity Book auf Seite 5.

_____   _____   _____   _____

_____   _____   _____   _____

green   red   yellow   blue   pink   brown   black   white

2 **So habe ich „Sally's rhyme" geübt:**

_____

_____

_____

_____

3 **Ich kann meine Telefonnummer auf Englisch nennen:**

What's your telephone number?

My telephone number is _____ .

4 **Das kann ich auch schon auf Englisch:**

Ich kann andere nach ihrer Telefonnummer fragen.   ○ ○ ○

Ich kann die Nummer verstehen und aufschreiben.   ○ ○ ○

Ich kann von 1 bis 10 zählen.   ○ ○ ○

Ich kann rückwärts von 10 bis 1 zählen.   ○ ○ ○

1 🖊 **Ich kann aufschreiben, was in meiner Schultasche ist:**

Hilfe findest du im Activity Book auf Seite 7.

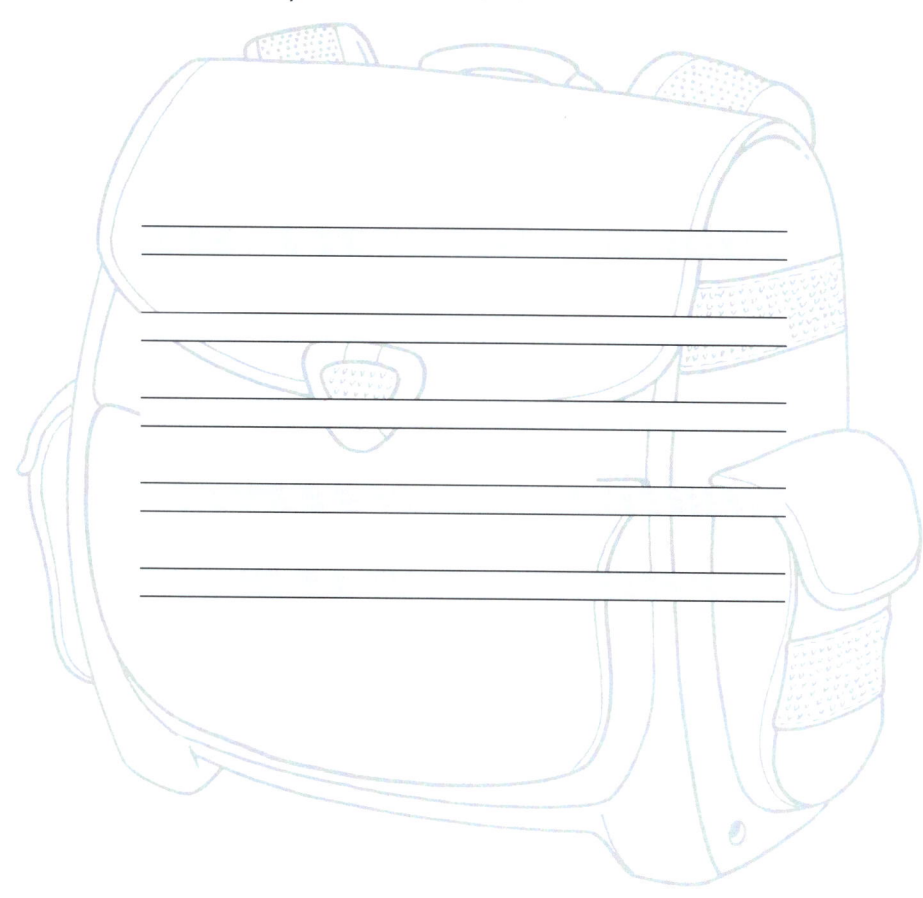

_____

_____

_____

_____

_____

_____

_____

_____

2 **Ich kann die Wörter in, on und under verwenden,**
um zu sagen, wo etwas ist: ✔

 ☐ under   ☐ on  ☐ in

3 **Ich kann auf Englisch etwas über meinen Schultag erzählen und**
aufschreiben (in welche Schule ich gehe usw.):

I go to _____

I'm in class _____

My teacher is _____

_____

_____

4 ✏ **Das weiß ich jetzt über die Schule in England:**
Hilfe findest du im Pupil's Book auf Seite 9.

5 **Das kann ich auch schon auf Englisch:**

Ich kann den „Schoolbag rap" mitsprechen.

Ich kann die Geschichte „Sally's school things" verstehen.

6 **Feedback**

Das hat mir in dieser Unit am meisten Spaß gemacht:

Das hat mir nicht gefallen:

1 🖊 **Diese Körperteile kann ich benennen:** ✔

Hilfe findest du im Activity Book auf den Seiten 9 und 10.

 ☐    ☐   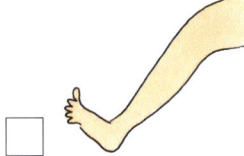 ☐   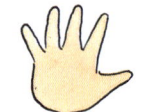 ☐

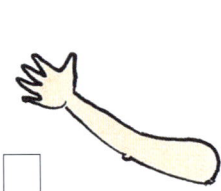 ☐   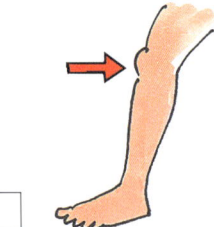 ☐   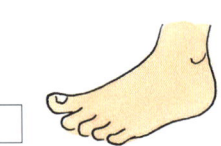 ☐

2 **Ich kann sagen, wie ich mich fühle:** ✔

Hilfe findest du im Activity Book auf den Seiten 11 und 12.

☐ I'm tired.

☐ I'm happy.

☐ I'm sad.

☐ I'm angry.

☐ I'm scared.

3 **Das kann ich auch schon auf Englisch:**

Ich kann das Lied „Head and shoulders" singen. ○ ○ ○

Ich kann den Comic „Ouch!" verstehen und vorspielen. ○ ○ ○

Ich kann die Geschichte „Get up, Susan!" verstehen
und die Bewegungen machen. ○ ○ ○

Ich kann sagen, wie ich mich fühle und auch warum. ○ ○ ○

Ich kann das Lied „If you're happy" singen. ○ ○ ○

4 🖉 **Ich habe eine eigene Strophe zum Lied „If you're happy"**
erfunden und vorgetragen. Das ist meine Strophe:

If you're _____ and you know it, _____

_____

_____

5 **Feedback**

Das hat mir in dieser Unit am meisten Spaß gemacht:

_____

_____

Das hat mir nicht gefallen:

_____

_____

Toys

1  **Ich kann diese Spielzeuge benennen:** ✔

Hilfe findest du im Activity Book auf den Seiten 13 und 14.

☐   ☐   ☐

☐   ☐   ☐

Ich kenne auch noch diese Spielzeuge:

_____

_____

2 **The fish who could wish**

Das hat mir geholfen, die Geschichte zu verstehen: ✔

☐ Ich habe mir vorgestellt, was in der Geschichte passiert.

☐ Ich habe beim Hören auf Wörter geachtet, die ich schon kenne.

☐ Ich habe mir die Bilder im Pupil's Book angesehen.

☐ Ich habe den Text im Pupil's Book mitgelesen.

3 Numbers

Ich kann bis 20 zählen.

Ich kann auch in Zehnerschritten weiterzählen (30, 40, …).

4 Ich kann fragen und sagen, wie viel etwas kostet:

Hilfe findest du im Pupil's Book auf Seite 15.

How much is the _____ ?

It's _____ pounds.

5 Feedback

Das hat mir in dieser Unit am meisten Spaß gemacht:

_____

_____

_____

_____

Das hat mir nicht gefallen:

_____

_____

_____

_____

Sally 3 Activity Book Förderheft © 2020 Cornelsen Verlag GmbH, Berlin

1 🖊 **Ich kann diese Kleidungsstücke benennen ✓ und aufschreiben:**
Hilfe findest du im Activity Book auf den Seiten 15 und 16.

 ☐

_____

 ☐

_____

 ☐

_____

 ☐

_____

 ☐

_____

 ☐

_____

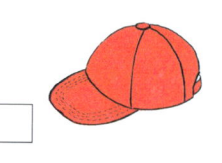 ☐

_____

cap   gloves   shoes   skirt   pullover   T-shirt   socks

2 **Das kann ich auch schon auf Englisch:**

Ich kann die Geschichte „Sally in the snow" verstehen.

Ich kann die Sätze den Bildern zuordnen:

Sally puts on her pullover.

Sally puts on her trousers.

Sally is wearing her scarf, her jacket and her gloves.

Sally 3 Activity Book Förderheft © 2020 Cornelsen Verlag GmbH, Berlin

3 💬 ✏️ **Ich kann sagen und aufschreiben, was ich heute anhabe:**

I'm wearing my _____

_____

jeans   T-shirt   pullover

4 **So merke ich mir neue Wörter:** ✔

☐ Ich stelle mir ein Bild dazu vor.

☐ Ich schreibe mir das Wort auf.

☐ Ich spreche mir das Wort ganz oft vor.

☐ Ich merke mir Sätze, in denen das Wort vorkommt.

5 **That's what I can do**

Hier ist Platz für deine Ideen. Du kannst ein Rätsel erfinden, etwas zum Thema „clothes"
schreiben oder malen, Bilder aus einem Katalog ausschneiden und beschriften usw.

1 🖊 **Ich kann die Wochentage in der richtigen Reihenfolge abschreiben:** Hilfe findest du im Activity Book auf Seite 17.

_____

_____

_____

_____

Monday Sunday Tuesday Friday Wednesday Thursday Saturday

2 🖊 **Ich kann mich mit jemandem verabreden:**

Can we meet on _____ ?

No, sorry. I can't.

And on _____ ?

Yes, great. Let's meet on _____ .

3 💬 **Ich kann sagen, wie das Wetter ist:** ✔

☐ In London it's windy.

☐ In Berlin it's cloudy.

☐ In Istanbul it's sunny.

☐ In Rome it's rainy.

4 **Das kann ich auch schon auf Englisch:**

Ich kann eine eigene Wettervorhersage schreiben.

○ ○ ○

Ich kann die Wettervorhersage vortragen.

○ ○ ○

Beim Vortragen achte ich auf diese Dinge besonders: ✔

☐ Ich spreche laut und deutlich.

☐ Ich schaue die Zuhörer an.

☐ Ich zeige Bilder.

Sally 3 Activity Book Förderheft © 2020 Cornelsen Verlag GmbH, Berlin

1 🖊 **Ich kann diese Geburtstagswörter benennen:** ✔

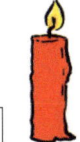 ☐    ☐    ☐   ☐

2 🖊 **Ich kann die Monatsnamen in der richtigen Reihenfolge abschreiben:** Hilfe findest du im Activity Book auf Seite 21.

_____

_____

_____

| January   April   March   February   August   June   September |
| May   July   December   November   October |

3 🖊 **Das kann ich auch schon auf Englisch:**

Ich kann jemanden fragen, wann er Geburtstag hat.

When's your _____ ?

Ich kann sagen, wann mein Geburtstag ist.

My birthday is in _____ .

Ich kann jemandem zum Geburtstag gratulieren.

_____ !

Ich kann eine Geburtstagseinladung schreiben.
Ich kann den Reim „Seasons" verstehen und mitsprechen.

1 🖊 **Ich kenne die Wörter für die Personen einer Familie:**

grandmother and grandfather

_____

_____

_____

_____

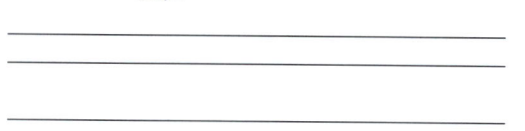

brother and sister   mother and father

2 🖊 **Ich kann eine Person (zum Beispiel einen Freund) beschreiben:**
Hilfe findest du im Activity Book auf Seite 22.

My friend is a _____

He/She is _____ years old.

He/She has got _____ hair and _____ eyes.

He/She is wearing a _____

3 **Das kann ich auch schon auf Englisch:**

Ich kann andere zu ihrer Familie befragen. 　　　　🟢 🟡 🔴

Ich kann sagen, wer zu meiner Familie gehört. 　　🟢 🟡 🔴

Ich kann die Geschichte „It's magic" verstehen. 　🟢 🟡 🔴

1 🖉 **Ich kann sagen, welche Getränke ich mag und welche nicht:**
Hilfe findest du im Activity Book auf Seite 25.

I like _____ .

I don't like _____ .

2 🖉 **Ich kenne auch noch diese kalten und heißen Getränke:**

Cold drinks: _____

Hot drinks: _____

Breakfast

1 💬 🖉 **Ich kann sagen und aufschreiben, was ich zum Frühstück**
esse: Hilfe findest du im Activity Book auf den Seiten 26 und 27.

For breakfast, I have _____

_____

2 🖉 **Ich kann mich beim Frühstück verständigen:**

Can I have the _____ , please?

Here you are.

Thank you.

Sally 3 Activity Book Förderheft © 2020 Cornelsen Verlag GmbH, Berlin

Fruit

1 💬✏️ **Ich kann sagen und aufschreiben, was in den Obstkörben ist:** Hilfe findest du im Activity Book auf Seite 28.

5 cherries, 2 _____   4 _____, 2 pears

1 _____ and 1 melon.   and 1 pineapple.

2 ✏️ **Ich kann ein Eis bestellen:**
Hilfe findest du im Activity Book auf Seite 29.

Hello, can I help you?

Yes, I'd like two scoops, please, _____ and _____.

Here you are. That's £2, please.

_____

_____

3 ✏️ **Ich kann sagen, was mein Lieblingseis ist:**

_____

_____

4 **Das kann ich auch schon auf Englisch:**

Ich kann das Gespräch von Phil und Emily
am Eisstand verstehen.

Ich kann den „Ice cream rock" singen.

Sally 3 Activity Book Förderheft © 2020 Cornelsen Verlag GmbH, Berlin

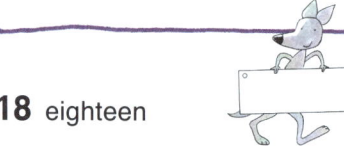

1 🖊 **Diese Tiere kann ich benennen** ✔ **und aufschreiben:**

Hilfe findest du im Activity Book auf Seite 31.

☐

_____

☐

_____

☐

_____

☐

_____

☐

_____

> cat   dog   fish   hamster   mouse

2 🖊 **Ich kann ein Haustier beschreiben.**

Hilfe findest du im Activity Book auf Seite 31.

My pet is a _____ .

Its name is _____ . It is _____

_____ .

3 **Das kann ich auch schon auf Englisch:**

Ich kann das Lied „Five little pets" singen.

Ich kann die Geschichte „Little dog lost" verstehen.

○ ○ ○

○ ○ ○

4 **Feedback**

Das hat mir in dieser Unit am meisten Spaß gemacht:

_____

Das hat mir nicht gefallen:

_____

Sally 3 Activity Book Förderheft © 2020 Cornelsen Verlag GmbH, Berlin

1 ✏️ **Ich kann Bilder und Wörter zuordnen:**

Hilfe findest du im Activity Book auf Seite 35.

| 1 ~~hen~~ |
| 2 horse |
| 3 sheep |
| 4 duck |
| 5 pig |
| 6 goose |
| 7 cow |

2 **Das kann ich auch schon auf Englisch:**

Ich kann die Geschichte „Clumsy the dog" verstehen.

Ich kann den „Bingo song" mitsingen.

3 **Alphabet**

Ich kann den „Alphabet rhyme" mitsprechen.

Ich kann das Alphabet aufsagen.

Ich kann einfache Wörter verstehen, die jemand buchstabiert.

Ich kann meinen Namen buchstabieren.

Sally 3 Activity Book Förderheft © 2020 Cornelsen Verlag GmbH, Berlin

4 I know an old lady ...

Ich kann die Geschichte „I know an old lady ..." verstehen.

Ich kann die Geschichte „I know an old lady ..." vorlesen.

Ich habe meine eigene Geschichte

„I know an old lady ..." geschrieben und kann sie vorlesen.

5 I know an old lady ...
Das hat mir geholfen, die Geschichte zu schreiben: ✔

☐ Ich habe die Wörter aus der Wörterbox genutzt.

☐ Ich habe die Wörter im Wörterbuch nachgeschlagen.

6 Animal rally

Diese Stationen konnte ich gut:

_____

_____

Bei dieser Station brauchte ich Hilfe:

_____

_____

7 Feedback

Das hat mir in dieser Unit am meisten Spaß gemacht:

_____

Das hat mir nicht gefallen:

_____

Hier sammle ich meine Lieblingswörter zu den verschiedenen Themen: Im letzten Feld kannst du eine eigene Überschrift wählen.

Colours and numbers	School
Clothes	Weather
Family and friends	Food and drinks

Body and feelings

Toys

Seasons and months

Around the year

Animals

Ich kenne mich gut aus und kann die folgenden Fragen beantworten: ✔

Where's Sally from?		
☐ England	AM	
☐ America	ER	
✔ Australia	EN	

Who brings the Easter eggs?		**What do you get for Christmas?**	
☐ Father Christmas	LG	☐ reindeer	SI
☐ Easter bunny	GL	☐ chimney	EH
☐ Sally	CA	☐ presents	IS

When is Halloween?		**What can you say on Halloween?**	
☐ on April 5th	HO	☐ Trick or treat!	SG
☐ on Friday	ME	☐ Spooky nights!	GE
☐ on October 31st	HI	☐ Good luck!	SH

Where does the Queen live?		**Who stands in front of Buckingham Palace?**	
☐ Loch Ness	OR	☐ the guards	A
☐ Buckingham Palace	RE	☐ Tim and Susan	M
☐ Germany	RA	☐ Madame Tussaud	S

What is not in London?

☐ double-decker bus	☐ London Eye	☐ Statue of Liberty
D	P	T

Trage die Buchstaben der richtigen Lösungen hier der Reihe nach ein.

E	N											!